MW01153542

# The Curated Home

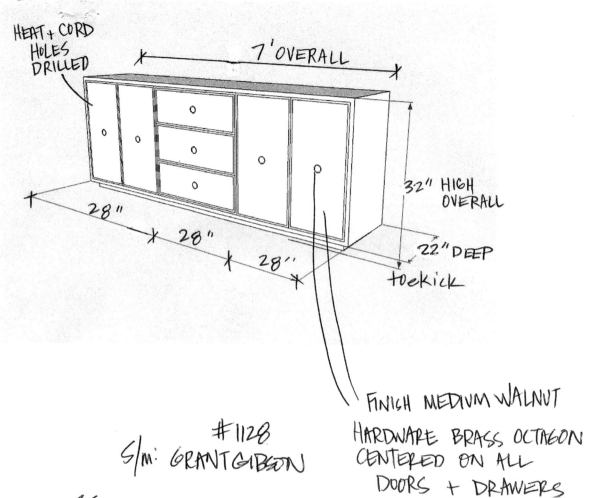

HEAT + CORD HOLES DRILLED

7' OVERALL

32" HIGH OVERALL

22" DEEP

toekick

28"

28"

28"

FINISH MEDIUM WALNUT
HARDWARE BRASS OCTAGON
CENTERED ON ALL
DOORS + DRAWERS

#1128
s/m: GRANT GIBSON

STYLE: KOENING CREDENZA

DIMS: 7' x 32"H x 22"D

FINISH: MEDIUM WALNUT + BRASS OCTAGON

DETAILS: HOLE FOR CORD + HEAT DRILLED ON
LEFT SIDE

\* RUSH MUST SHIP MONDAY 10/10 \*

# The Curated Home

## A FRESH TAKE ON TRADITION

GRANT K. GIBSON

Principal Photography by Kathryn MacDonald

**GIBBS SMITH**
TO ENRICH AND INSPIRE HUMANKIND

First Edition
22 21 20 19 18      5 4 3 2 1

Text © 2018 Grant K. Gibson
Principal photography © 2018 Kathryn MacDonald except
page 8 © Caitlin Flemming
page 17, 58, 147, 176 (left) © Peggy Wong
page 24, 49 ,66, 111 (left), 134 (left), back cover © Brittany
    Ambridge for Condé Nast
page 87 (left) © Kelly Ishikawa
page 206 © Margot Hartford

All rights reserved. No part of this book may be reproduced
by any means whatsoever without written permission from
the publisher, except brief portions quoted for purpose of
review.

Published by
Gibbs Smith
P.O. Box 667
Layton, Utah 84041

1.800.835.4993 orders
www.gibbs-smith.com

Designed by Sheryl Dickert
Printed and bound in China

Gibbs Smith books are printed on either recycled, 100%
post-consumer waste, FSC-certified papers or on paper
produced from sustainable PEFC-certified forest/con-
trolled wood source. Learn more at www.pefc.org.

Library of Congress Cataloging-in-Publication Data

Names: Gibson, Grant K., author.
Title: The curated home : a fresh take on tradition / Grant K.
Gibson.
Description: Layton, Utah : Gibbs Smith, [2018]
Identifiers: LCCN 2018000338 | ISBN 9781423647898
(jacket less hardcover)
Subjects: LCSH: Interior decoration. | Gibson, Grant K.
Classification: LCC TX311 .G48 2018 | DDC 747--dc23
LC record available at https://lccn.loc.gov/2018000338

To M + W

# Contents

# Introduction

I'm sure you've heard this before—a home and its décor tell the story of its inhabitants. Similarly, I believe that the portfolio of an interior designer says a lot about who he or she is. A room doesn't just convey aesthetic principles and preferences. It can overtly or subtly display the lessons a designer has learned over the years, destinations visited (and loved), under-the-radar shops discovered, and so much more.

This book, which highlights projects from my career, could be described as a visual representation of my lived experiences. It is my personal journey told through the lens of my favorite design projects and my travels near and far. My hope is that after reading along, you'll be more confident embarking on your *own* design journey. After all, you share the story of your life when you invite others into your home. The way you use furniture, colors, textures, art, and even the scent of your home all convey who you are. If you think about your home as an extension of your personality, then who knows better than you what it should look like and feel like?

In the following pages, I'll share with you how I approach my projects and provide insights into how you can work with a design professional, while also imparting ideas that you can apply in your own home. It's not only about practical tips—how to display objects from travels, what to look for when making furniture purchases, and the type of paints that work best in a particular room—but also how to think like an interior designer. If you're wondering if I talk about the importance of dimmers, just like every other design book, you'd be correct. (Because they're that important!)

One of the most important lessons I ever learned occurred when I was asked to participate in my first design show house in San Francisco. Opening night happened to fall on my twenty-fifth birthday, which is what I like to think of as the launch of my career. I was young and intimidated by all of the veteran designers. I was responsible for the smallest room in the house, and I filled it with flea market

above: Wesley, an honorary Grant K. Gibson Interior Design employee, reviews concepts for a project.

finds since that was all I could afford. The room was entitled "A Gentleman's Retreat." I feared being the laughing stock when the doors opened. All of the other designers had hired the best decorative painters in town and had spent thousands of dollars on things such as custom silk curtains. I had been on my hands and knees refinishing the hardwood floors myself and painting the walls with a few gallons from the neighborhood hardware store. Despite its humble nature, the room was a success and I started to receive small interior jobs which turned into larger jobs. The lesson I learned? Trust your instincts. This has been a returning mantra for me.

I grew up in the Los Feliz area of Los Angeles in the '80s. As an only child, I would often accompany my parents to dinner parties and museums as well as on trips—experiences that would later shape my own environment as well as those I conjure up for my clients. I also spent countless hours in my bedroom, letting my imagination run wild. But I wasn't playing with stuffed animals or Legos. No, I was thinking about how the wood paneling would look so much better painted white (it did) and wondering if there were beautiful hardwood floors beneath the carpeting (there were, and I successfully campaigned for the floors to be refinished while I was away at summer camp). It seems I've spent my life reimagining and rearranging things. Sometimes, it's just in my head; other times, I'm lucky enough to execute my ideas. (For example, as soon as I get to the summer cottage I rent in Maine, I take down the curtains, move the furniture, and banish to the spare bedroom chairs and lamps that offend my sensibilities.)

My mother worked in fashion when I was young, which perhaps explains my love of fabrics and bringing together different textures and patterns in

a cohesive vision. But how she spent her off-duty hours has had an even stronger influence on me: she loved to cook. If I weren't an interior designer, no doubt I would be working in a kitchen somewhere. I'm comfortable experimenting, and that goes for my cooking as well as my interior design work. It's a mind-set that I often suggest to my clients when they're overthinking something or getting hung up on one particular idea that pushes them a bit. If you don't like the way certain flavors are working together in a dish, you can add and subtract until it's to your liking. The same is often true of design.

My father's influence on my career path is more straightforward: he has a passion for restoring houses. I spent countless weekends on job sites and tagging along as he worked on projects. I can also blame him for my obsession with real estate and antique stores. When I was twelve, he let me join him on a business trip to New York City. I fondly remember passing the days exploring the city's great museums while he worked. I think, like so many people, I fell in love with

Comments (Optional) *Grant is an enthusiastic learner. He has formed positive relationships with his peers. He enjoys expressing himself in art.*

the energy of the city and I was fascinated with the liveliness of it all. Eight years later, I returned—this time, to live on the Upper West Side and pursue a career in interior design.

But there was more to my education. As a struggling, dyslexic teenager, I literally escaped the difficulties I had in school—academically and socially—by traveling. Discovering places like the Sir John Soane's Museum in London, exploring Rome, and spending a summer in Sweden allowed for self-learning about architecture, art, and furnishings from various eras. Additionally, I gained an appreciation for different cultures—their foods and music, for example. My friends often joke that I am usually planning my next trip before my current trip is even complete. Travel is a luxury, I know, and not everyone can jump on a plane whenever wanderlust kicks in. I guess what interests me about travel is the sense of adventure and the discovery of new cultures, from how people live to the architecture to the aromas of the markets frequented by locals. My design aesthetic will forever be intertwined with influences from my travels. Inspiration from travel and using items I bring back provides a fresh spin on my own existing living space and those I help create for my clients.

Today, all of these memories—from my childhood to adolescence to early adulthood—are reflected in my portfolio. The tiles in Portugal, the colors of the trees and water in Maine, strolling

the streets of Paris, and many other travel experiences have been used for inspiration.

I believe that a home should speak to its inhabitants' life and loves. Yes, a client may be hiring me for my expertise and eye, but ultimately, what we create together is tailored to him or her. The best homes are usually the ones that feel as if they haven't been decorated; people can't tell if a designer's hand has been there at all. This is one of the reasons I love what I do. I collaborate with a myriad of clients, using a multitude of design styles. Each project should feel unique and, at the end, really reflect who actually lives in the home. The treasures that fill your home—collected by you and meaningful to you— speak to your personality. Keep this in mind as you move forward with your next decorating endeavor to give you confidence in your decisions. Now, what are you waiting for? Let's get going . . .

opposite top: My first day of kindergarten at Franklin Avenue Elementary in Los Angeles. (Look at those bangs!)

opposite center: This is one of my favorite memories—after brunch at a friend's house in Santa Barbara with Julia Child.

top: An excerpt from an elementary school report card. "Grant is an enthusiastic learner. He has formed positive relationships with his peers. He enjoys expressing himself in art."

center: Kissing a giraffe during a trip to Kenya in 2013.

# Primer

Working with clients is a bit like dating—you really have to get to know the person you are going to spend time with. Before embarking on any project, I sit down with my clients and ask them questions—a lot of them. This helps me determine budgets and styles they might like and not like, and learn what the overall goals are for the way they want the spaces in their house to function. The following are a few things to consider before designing or simply tweaking your décor, as well as things to consider before making any purchases.

## DETERMINE YOUR STYLE

How do you want a space to feel? Here's a trick to help you home in on your style: take a look at your closet. Do you prefer tailored pieces or do you prefer looser and more comfortable items? Do you gravitate toward certain colors or patterns? Another way to help you determine your style is to think of key words that define how you want a space to feel. Traditional, formal, elegant? Playful, humorous, inviting? Monochromatic, streamlined, modern?

Take note of design inspirations in every facet of life. I often use these as a starting point to discuss with clients. Even if you don't regularly leaf through the latest design magazines, something has certainly put the design bug in you if you're reading this book. Recall a hotel in which you've stayed or restaurant in which you've dined that particularly struck your fancy. Perhaps it was a minimal interior from your trip to Japan or a clubby bar in New York furnished with worn leather chairs.

## FIGURE OUT WHAT YOU DON'T LIKE

It is a lot easier for people to express what they do not like. By putting dislikes into the equation, we can eliminate some things and narrow in on others. For example, a bold large-scale print might remind you of something in your childhood that you do not want to see in your own space. Or a wingback chair might bring back memories of being sent to time-outs for pulling your sister's hair. Likewise, a certain color might evoke feelings of a past design trend that you aren't eager to repeat. These memories and reactions are very personal and individual, but also define our tastes.

## THINK ABOUT OPTIMAL POSITIONING

What is the optimal place to position yourself in a room? Where does the light come in, or where are the views best? How does the space look from the spot where you will likely be sitting (or standing, as is the case perhaps in the kitchen) most of the time? This line of questioning may help you decide on furniture purchases and placements. For example, you may want to avoid walking into a room to immediately face the back of a tall piece of furniture, such as a high-backed chair or sofa. Lower profile seating (or a bench with no back) will make a space feel more open and inviting when you enter. Do you want your desk or computer facing a window or the door? What do you want to see when you first wake up—a fireplace, a window, a favorite painting? In addition to thinking about how furniture pieces relate to one another and the room, you'll want to think about the traffic flow: how people enter, exit, and navigate the room. For example, in a living room, make sure people can easily get in and out of the seating group without having to awkwardly tango around a side table.

opposite: Using a variety of dark blues helped to achieve a moody, club-like atmosphere in this library.

top: My travels to India have provided infinite inspiration.

center: Samples are important to get a feel (literally) for a fabric—and determine the proper balance of textures in a room.

bottom: Picking the perfect shade of a color requires many swatches.

## BUILD AROUND YOUR SPACE

Space planning, which impacts scale, is essential. People often use furniture that is too large or too small for a space. I like to blame a certain retail company for the large-scale furnishings that saturate interiors today. Build around the furniture that you actually have space for. Think about the balance of a space. For larger rooms, consider establishing zones for different activities: a seating area that is conducive to conversation; another area for television viewing; a work area with a desk or table for projects or games. Even though I love symmetry, you can make things feel too contrived when you make everything symmetrical. Think about the visual weight and distribution to balance out a space. Proportion and scale are key to any design.

## LET THERE BE LIGHT

There should be more than one lighting source in every room. Overhead lights provide the overall function of lighting a space, but they can be harsh. Layer your lighting to include table lamps, candles, and dimmers (even in bathrooms) to create the right mood. Task lighting allows for focused lighting, creating zones within spaces, allowing for directional function. If you are installing overhead lighting as part of a remodel, make sure the junction boxes can support the weight of the light fixture.

When purchasing antique sconces or other light fixtures it is important to think about backplates and wiring. If you have the luxury of adding electrical receptacles in the floor, this will reduce the volume of cords. Develop a furniture plan first, so that cords can be hidden under large pieces of furniture rather than in a pathway. You might want to work with a lighting designer or consult with your architect or contractor for advice, since floor joists and weight-bearing walls can pose their own set of problems. Consider the locations of thermostats, light switches, and alarms so they are not focal points in a room. By planning the placement, you can also better accommodate art on the walls. For major art walls, consider using spotlights to highlight and wash over the art.

## SAMPLE YOUR PAINT

Paint selection is one of the most important and cost-effective decisions you can make. Proper paint choices harmoniously connect spaces. Consider the house as a whole. You risk creating disjointed rooms if you paint one room at time. Take into account how colors affect our mood. Some colors make people feel happy, calm, or even agitated. I have been known to paint interior doors a bold black for a contrast against crisp white walls.

Sample actual paint colors on your walls when looking at options. Observe them in natural light, morning light, and at night. Often a go-to color that worked well for one project will not work for another. What might work at your friend's home might

*As for finish details or sheens, I am a fan of flat paint. It creates a chalky feel that makes the walls recess. This does come with its own issues, as it shows fingerprints or marks from daily activities, such as the vacuum cleaner bumping into the wall. My solution is to have a small Tupperware container and a paintbrush in the pantry. This allows for easy touch-ups, which are just part of everyday life.*

not work at your home. The chips at the paint store are a helpful starting point, but what looks good on paper might not translate into your interior. With white paints, try a handful of different hues on the wall and pay special attention to the undertones. They can have touches of pinks, blues, or yellows. The outside surroundings strongly affect the temperature of the light. The vegetation and the sky can create reflections of greens and blues on your interior walls.

## MIX HIGH AND LOW PRICE POINTS

Pedigree doesn't necessarily mean better (whether it be art, furniture, or dogs). Consider an "unknown" artist or designer and buy based on shape, comfort, and how the art or furniture works for you and your needs. The most humble objects can have the most soul and be the most beautiful thing in a room. Do not be afraid to mix high and low price points. Not everything must be precious to be important. The opposite can be said with splurging on something that you really love.

## DO NOT DESIGN BY COMMITTEE

Seeking the opinion of all your friends and family is asking for trouble. If you are not working with a design professional—someone who takes the time to get to know you and can successfully express your ideas—pair yourself with a stylish friend or two and ask for their opinions. But you do not need to start asking everyone in your child's carpool group. If you must, consult a few people who truly understand you and your lifestyle, and whose taste you admire. I had a client who was always seeking a second opinion on fabrics or other design elements. This is like asking my dry cleaner his thoughts on what color to paint my living room. While my dry cleaner may know how to remove a stain from my dress shirt, I wouldn't ask him for decorating advice. And I'm perfectly fine if he doesn't consult with me about the best methods for removing lipstick or red wine.

## START FROM THE GROUND UP

Design can be overwhelming. People often want to know where exactly to start. For any room, I usually suggest that you begin from the ground up: Decide on the floor covering. It doesn't matter if you want or have hardwood floors, area rugs, tile or stone, or wall-to-wall carpeting. Thinking about your floor first will dictate how other pieces are layered in the space. If you select a neutral tone or natural fiber without a lot of pattern or color, you have more options with colors or upholstery. If you start with an antique rug, you can draw colors from the rug to formulate a color palette. It is important to plan these things in tandem, otherwise you end up with the circus effect: too many things going on without the space as a whole functioning in unison. Starting with a sofa or upholstered chairs limits your style immediately.

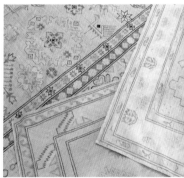

top: An antelope motif adds whimsy to a staircase.

center: I always recommend testing out multiple area rugs— if possible—to see how they work in your home.

bottom: Selecting a hardwood floor stain often entails trial and error.

There is more flexibility with something like an area rug with dozens or even hundreds of possibilities. This is where you have options and can then start to layer pieces. It is a much easier approach to make your final floor covering decision first, and then layer.

## CHOOSE YOUR FABRIC

This may sound counterintuitive, but when choosing textiles, think about opposites and contrasts. Opposites attract. This goes for colors, patterns, and textures. An assortment of fabrics helps create a balanced room that gives the eye—as well as the hand—some variation. Mix linen with its organic woven quality with plush velvet and smooth leather. Not only can they all work in the same space, but you can even combine them in one piece—perhaps an armchair with a base wrapped in leather and cushions upholstered in velvet. For a more understated mix that still allows for some contrast, pair solid linen with a subtle herringbone linen; the latter is a quiet way to inject pattern. I absolutely love it when someone walks into an interior I designed and touches the back of a sofa or picks up an accent pillow. Design is as much tactile as it is visual.

## GO THE EXTRA YARD

If you're reupholstering a piece of furniture, don't overlook outdoor fabrics, which are durable and usually easy to clean. Clients are often surprised how frequently I utilize outdoor fabrics inside the home. These fabrics can achieve the look of linen or velvet while repelling moisture and protecting against stains. People like to blame children and pets for destroying furniture, but adult guests at parties can do just as much damage. I will never forget when my dear aunt spilled a glass of red wine over my brand new linen sofa. If you are ordering yardage for a sofa or chair, consider adding a few extra yards (tuck this away in a drawer or closet) in case there's a situation down the road and the fabric may no longer be available. It is much cheaper to recover a cushion than an entire piece of furniture! Think of

above: Our upholstery work-room at the ready with bolts of fabric.

center: Spreading out swatches for a living room concept helps me visualize how the elements complement one another.

this as an insurance policy. If this ever happens to you, you can give me a call to thank me.

## TAKE YOUR TIME

So many options can be overwhelming, for sure. How do you know where to look and what to look for? Whether you're browsing flea markets, high-end showrooms, or chain stores like IKEA, look for classic and timeless lines. Invest in the best quality that you can afford for your budget. And think about design as the evolution of a process. This can be done over time. Sure, you can go out and decorate your home in a weekend, but what fun is that? Rushing to furnish a home can lead to desperation purchases that may not be very well thought-out. Here are two reasons why you should take it slow. First, it allows you to shop for the best pricing as well as spread your costs over a longer period of time (making it hurt less). Second, it gives you a chance to discover items that have interest and a story. (They aren't always at the first—or second or fifth—store you walk into.) I try to buy the best quality that I can. This isn't just for interior purchases, but even for a pair a shoes or a cashmere sweater. When taken care of, these items can last for years. How often do we look into our closets and think, *Wow, I have had this for more than ten years and still love it.*

## DISREGARD TRENDS

Lastly, throw trends right out the window. This year's look may not be "in" next year. Let's not even talk about what your hair looked like in high school. The same wisdom should be applied to interiors.

The kitchen in the private residence at Napa's Nine Suns Winery includes Fireclay tiles, arranged in a unique herringbone pattern that incorporates two shades of orange.

# The Foyer

It's cliché, but true: You never get a second chance to make a first impression. Well, yes, you could redecorate—but you understand the point here. The foyer sets the tone. It is the first thing you see when you enter, whether you have had a good or bad day. It should be both visually pleasing and functional. Is there a spot to hang coats and scarves? Is there an organized place for keys, sunglasses, and mail? Baskets, trays, and bowls for tables work wonders at making things seem more organized.

In this entryway, a Christopher Spitzmiller lamp sits atop an antique French chest of drawers— an elegant receptacle to keep keys and other knickknacks handy, yet out of sight.

opposite: A simple round mirror is understated, allowing the floating marble console to be the star.

left: An octagon-shaped mirror and Giacometti table lamp pair well with the geometric design on the Moroccan rug.

## MAKE THE MOST OF YOUR SPACE

Does the foyer have enough light so that you can actually see yourself? Lanterns, decorative lamps, or sconces are key. Mirrors can be functional for checking your lipstick or ensuring that there isn't spinach in your teeth before you leave the house. Mirrors can also expand the space, giving the optical illusion that the space is larger than it is.

## CONSIDER YOUR GUESTS

Are you a shoeless house? If so, is there a place for guests to leave their shoes, and maybe even exchange for slippers? If you are a shoeless house, which I understand completely, please advise your guests ahead of time. This will forewarn them to wear respectable socks or easy-to-remove shoes. Consider a chair or a bench where someone may sit to remove or put on their shoes, so there is no awkward hopping about. At least make sure your guests have a half table or banister to hold on to before you set a hard and fast rule for shoelessness.

Is the foyer large enough to greet and mingle a bit with guests? If so, is there a place to offer them a drink? If your home has more than one entrance—like a garage or a mud room—think about how you can make these spaces special to both guests and yourself on a daily basis. I once had a very tiny studio apartment that had a disproportionate foyer compared to the rest of the diminutive square footage. This allowed for a table and chairs to be placed in the foyer for dinner parties. Think about how to make a space work for you and how to make it your own.

right: When you choose such a beautiful tile, there's no reason to cover it up with a rug!

opposite top: An inspiration shot from my trip to Turkey—proof that ceramic tiles stand the test of time.

opposite center: Lay out your tiles before grouting to ensure that you love the configuration.

opposite bottom: The same tile functions equally well in this sunroom.

*If you want to make a decorative statement, a foyer is a good place to opt for a bold wallpaper or unexpected color. Taking a chance in this smaller space that you pass through is less overwhelming than, say, a living room or bedroom where you tend to spend hours at a time.*

opposite: A single piece of furniture—like this custom fuchsia Campaign-style chest—can enliven an entry, but can easily be swapped out if a client's tastes change.

left: Opting for a bold pattern in the entry makes for an unforgettable first impression.

above: A yellow door in Maine stopped me in my tracks—and put a smile on my face. I knew I needed to inject this happy color in a client's home!

left: A stool is not only practical, but fills a visual void beneath the table.

right: In this home, the client requested a spot to sit for putting on shoes. The painting defines the area, so the bench doesn't seem like an afterthought floating on its own.

An upholstered bench provides opportunity to add pattern to a space.

# Living Spaces

For many of us, the living spaces—which I define as the living rooms, family rooms, dens, and home offices—are where we spend most of our hours when we are at home and not sleeping. Plan your interiors for how *you* live on a daily basis and not for the occasional guest. Create functionality and comfort for you and your family first.

For this sunroom—which the client envisioned as a sanctuary—we opted for a soothing palette with green accents that echo the surroundings.

## START WITH THE LARGEST PIECE IN THE ROOM

Avoid getting overwhelmed: Focus on a key piece as a jumping-off point. You can start with the flooring (see page 15 for more details on flooring tips). Or start with a sofa (or dining table)—as they are the larger statement pieces of a room—and then layer around them. I tend to go for neutral colors for the more significant elements in a room, then I have some fun with bolder accents. For example, rather than upholstering your sofa in animal print, a solid neutral fabric as a base can allow for more flexibility when you want to refresh the look of a room later. It's much easier (and less expensive) to swap out a patterned pillow than an entire sofa!

above: Among my many Paris flea market scores is this pair of cocktail tables, comprised of black glass and metal.

right: The reflective quality and shape of the tables—which now reside in my living room—pop against the navy sofa. Every time I walk into the room and see them, it brings back memories of my trip to Paris. And having a pair of small tables, instead of one large table, allows more flexibility when I'm entertaining.

left: In a San Francisco bachelor pad, the Eames lounge chair and ottoman were uphol-stered in gray linen to add more texture.

above: The year-long restoration included bringing back architectural elements that were in alignment with the home's original Edwardian character.

## ALLOW FOR FLEXIBLE SEATING

If things appear to be too perfectly arranged, people hover uncomfortably, are afraid to sit, and are hesitant to move a chair or pillows to get comfortable. Flexible seating groups are for real life, different from what we see in movies, glossy design magazines, or even this book. One of my favorite ways to create extra seating is with benches or stools. They are probably not going to be used daily, so they can be tucked under a console table and easily brought out when visitors arrive. Be realistic with yourself and plan accordingly. Where will everyone sit when it is your turn to host your book club? Consider spaces with alternative seating arrangements. Why not have a space that is all chairs? There isn't a law saying you must have a sofa and chairs in a space.

opposite: The configuration of this seating is inviting, beckoning you to come in and stay for awhile. The softness of the English roll arm chairs' curves lend a sculptural quality to the room.

above: In this home, whose residents include four children and a black Lab, the light-weight stools function as both seating and a footrest.

top: Hands down, blue is favorite color with my clients—to whom I often show this photo (depicting a door in Maine) as a good jumping-off point.

center: The hand-painted surfaces at Jaipur's City Palace (which dates back to 1729) are proof that blue-and-white patterns are timeless.

bottom: Anchored by Adirondack chairs painted in a fun hue, the view is the focal point in this favorite spot in Maine.

left: To mix up the fabrics in this room, the seating is upholstered in various fabrics—mohair, cashmere, and silk—that share a luxurious quality and suggest a formal atmosphere. The large-scale photograph is by Richard Misrach.

above: The neutral palette draws you into the artwork, a Candida Höfer photograph of Buenos Aires' Teatro Nacional Cervantes.

I am going to channel Miss
Manners here. As a host, I
think that it is important to
always give your guests the
most comfortable places to sit.
This might mean that you are
perched on the arm of a sofa
or on a bench or dining room
chair pulled in from another
room, while your guests sit
on the sofa or your favorite
armchair. I also like to situate
myself as close to the entrance
as possible, allowing me an
easy escape to refill glasses of
wine, stir the risotto, or simply
escape for a moment from a
loquacious visitor.

opposite top: Opposites attract—that is indeed the case with these two seemingly disparate motifs: the traditional Greek key rug and the wild tiger-print stool.

opposite bottom: By visiting our upholstery workroom in Los Angeles, we can try out pieces before they're completed to help ensure that they're comfortable.

left: The barrel backs on these gingham-covered Swedish chairs pick up on the arched window in a Spanish-Mediterranean home.

## BE MINDFUL OF SCALE

Let's talk about size. What is the saying about measuring things twice? There is a huge trend toward overscale, which does have its place. Just make sure that the piece of furniture you are considering will fit in the space that you desire, as well as down hallways and through door frames.

Many people don't realize that there is scale to light fixtures. Finding a style you love is one thing, but the scale of the same fixture can look completely different depending on the space. If it's oversized in a room, it is a statement piece. If it is installed in a much grander place—with more square footage and higher ceilings—it can appear delicate (and perhaps more than one fixture would be wise).

above: We borrowed this painting from the Walter Kuhlman Gallery so the client could live with it for a while to determine whether the size was right for the wall above his fireplace.

My firm has been known to hire cranes to move larger pieces of art and furniture through windows.

opposite top: A custom Lucite coffee table that hovers over a tufted ottoman offers the ultimate in flexibility.

opposite bottom: We turned a previously underutilized large landing area into a highly functional office with ample book storage.

left: For a client in San Francisco, we designed this entire room around his Steinway Concert Grand Piano, including seating for friends to relax and enjoy his musical talents.

With an open floor plan, rugs can serve to delineate the living and dining areas. In this case, I placed a Moroccan rug atop a jute rug; they're both neutral and composed of natural textures. The subdued pairing allows the art and bright accents—like the peacock blue chair—to take center stage.

The inspiration for the channeling in this sofa came from two unexpected sources: the Museo Rufino Tamayo in Mexico City and a hot-air balloon ride in Africa. This Bradley Duncan piece is made of pegs; the three dimensional art adds interest.

## INVEST IN THE SOFA

When it comes to purchasing chairs and sofas (please do not call it a couch, which hurts my ears), this is not the place to "cheap out." Invest in buying something that is the best quality that you can afford. But remember that quality and cost are not exactly synonymous, so do not simply opt for the most expensive thing you can find. People often make the mistake of buying "placeholder sofas," meaning that they are less well made and will eventually (most likely sooner than later) wear out. I am no math genius, but if you add up all of those cheap sofas you've gone through over the years, you will most likely exceed the price of investing in a quality piece one time. Thank you to my third grade teacher, Mrs. Marshall, who told me math would come in handy someday.

Key furniture that is well made can last a lifetime. Consider how past generations recovered pieces rather than replacing them. I also advise people to not buy furniture in sets. There needs to be balance in a space. If your sofa happens to have a skirt, make sure that the chairs do not or vice versa. Similarly, you don't want to have too many wooden legs that all look the same, or have everything the same size or scale or even upholstered in the same material. You can create a far more interesting, layered, and balanced room by keeping these rules in mind.

opposite: The Hunt Slonem artwork was painted with diamond dust, infusing shimmer and sparkle into the piece, which is especially dramatic at night.

left: Chairs that previously belonged to the client's grandmother were enlivened with pink leather.

below: A client's favorite local restaurant is appointed with Fermob bistro-style tables and chairs. We used this color inspiration to achieve a similar feeling in her home.

## INSTILL A SENSE OF WHIMSY

I recently had a client request that her home look like that of her best friend, who also happened to be a client of mine. Yikes! It is important to individualize your space and allow it to be unique to you. While you should absolutely pull inspiration from magazines or a friend's home, think of those things as only a starting point. Quirky details and a sense of humor, fantasy, or whimsy add to making a space feel personalized. Incorporating something surprising or unexpected will make it yours.

above: Pillows made of Quadrille fabrics punch up a playroom without sacrificing style; the motifs are not overly juvenile, so they don't need to be tossed aside as the kids grow up.

right: A gilded frame elevates artwork by the client's four-year-old, and is juxtaposed with antiqued mirror-backed built-in shelving.

right: A bouquet of flowers—even of simple white tulips—introduces a fresh silhouette (not to mention height, color, and texture) to a tablescape.

opposite: On this coffee table, I combined various materials—quartz, alabaster, and porcelain—to create continuity with the creamy palette of the room.

## CREATE PERSONAL VIGNETTES

Coffee tables, occasional tables, and end tables can be used for decorative vignettes. They are useful ways to beautifully display books, flowers, or other collected objects. Just don't overdo it with the styling and make sure to allow for space to put a drink. Offer coasters for guests so they can feel at ease.

opposite: The peony is undoubtedly my go-to flower. Its simple elegance requires little else to liven up a cocktail table.

above: Succulents floating in a shallow vessel are an unexpected choice that achieves a sophisticated look.

*Remember, things do
not always have to
coordinate. It is all about
juxtaposition and creating
a conversation between
objects. Consider mixing
heirloom furniture with
contemporary pieces.
Mixing eras is like a good
cocktail: You don't want to
be heavy-handed with any
one ingredient.*

opposite: The colors in a Peggy Wong photo perfectly complement a nearby travertine-topped table.

left: When designing a space, I like to think about how it looks from every angle. For example, in the doorway of this living room, the wingback chair is a sculptural greeting.

## REMEMBER WHO LIVES HERE

One of my clients had a small two-bedroom apartment. She worked from home and was cramped in the guest room with a very tiny desk and a queen-sized bed that overpowered the space. When asked how often she had guests, she replied maybe ten nights a year. I asked her why she was willing to sacrifice her own comfort 355 days a year to make her guests comfortable for just a few days. The queen-sized bed was removed, and a large desk and a small sofa bed were brought in. This allowed my client much more space for her day-to-day living, and when a guest did arrive, she had the perfect place for them to spend a few days.

left: On a day-to-day basis, this tailored room is an ideal venue for reading and working. A pull-out sofa allows the home office to easily double as a guest room.

overlay: The massive Peggy Wong photograph of Hong Kong's Victoria Harbour was custom printed to fit perfectly within the room's molding detail.

# Dining Spaces

Dining rooms take on many forms—from spacious rooms to nooks off the kitchen. No matter the size or style, a dining space is meant to be a place to gather for everyday meals and special occasions.

My fondest childhood memories are with my family in our dining room. White roses freshly cut from the garden were a common sight, while different tablescapes were conjured for varied occasions, from birthday parties to elegant Saturday evening dinners. There always seemed to be an event or holiday being celebrated in the dining room.

Some clients are fearless, as evidenced by the Ellie Cashman large-scale floral wallpaper, green leather Saarinen Executive dining chairs, and Apparatus chandelier.

## CURATE A HOME BAR

When guests arrive, one of the first questions you'll likely ask them is: Would you like something to drink? A drinks station or self-serve bar is a great addition to any dining room. I notice that guests find this concept inviting and immediately feel at home. This also helps the host (you) avoid getting overwhelmed. You don't have to keep playing bartender or juggle multiple drink orders. If you don't have a designated bar area, even a spot on a low bookshelf will do. Or, create a temporary space on a credenza or side table.

opposite: A self-service bar at the entry sets the mood that this is a casual, fun residence whose occupants don't take themselves too seriously.

above: Having a clutter-free dining surface allows flexibility in how a table is used—in this case, for wine and cheese.

right: It's hard to go wrong with this classic Pierre Frey blue-and-white textile. Here, I've married it with rattan chargers, vintage silverware with bamboo handles, and Bordallo Pinheiro cabbage plates.

opposite: Place settings aren't always necessary for a soirée. Simply putting out plates, glasses, napkins, and silverware can make guests feel more at home (which I love).

## HOST A DINNER PARTY

I love to cook and entertain. My personal style of entertaining is very casual. I prefer to have everything set and ready to go long before guests arrive. Laughing over a bottle of wine and a prepared meal at someone's home is much more intimate and personal than eating out. You do not need to reserve your wedding china or fancy napkins for a special occasion. Instead, mix these pieces into your regular rotation. One of the best dinner parties I ever attended was with take-out Chinese served on the host's grandmother's fine china. You could also bring out that textile that you acquired on a trip for meals such as these. Maybe the tablecloth or napkins are a bit more colorful than your day-to-day interior. Taking them out of their storage spot to actually use and creating a special environment for you and your guests is part of the fun. A pack of tealights from IKEA and glass votive holders can also give you a lot of bang for your buck. A sprinkling of these around a table tricks your guests into thinking that you have done something special. The light is also very flattering. I often set up a buffet of sorts with stacks of dishes, napkins, and silverware. Many of these pieces are from collections that I started years ago. I love reminiscing about where I purchased pieces and sharing the details with my guests. There is usually a happy memory associated with each item.

*My parents kept linens, place mats, and a myriad of other decorative options in the butler's pantry, and I was often lucky enough to be put in charge of devising just the right look. When I think back on my childhood dining room, I have vivid memories of toasts, laughing, and great conversations. This is no doubt why I still find eating at home more inviting than going out. It seems so personal to welcome guests into your home, and to create an experience uniquely for them. Perhaps the idea of more formal dinners is not as common today as it was a couple of decades ago, but I do know a lot of people that still enjoy this tradition. In these modern times, it remains a wonderful way to connect with others (no cell phones, please).*

Never underestimate the power of foliage. Don't feel like you have to bring in an elaborate centerpiece for your next dinner party. As these images demonstrate, something simple—a collection of anemones, a single succulent, or a grouping of eucalyptus—is all you need.

above: The wooden table with a live edge adds an organic feeling to this dining room. Oversized dining chairs provide comfortable seating, inviting guests to lounge for hours.

opposite: I designed these Parsons-style tables in oak with a cerused finish for MacRostie Winery. The benches make for flexible seating. I love playing with different textures and materials in a space—in this case, concrete floors, leather benches, and oak make for an interesting tactile experience.

*It may not seem like a big deal, but trust me, you want dimmer switches. They are well worth the investment. You can install dimmers for overhead lighting as well as convert any lamp with plug-in dimmers sold at hardware stores or online. Soft light sets the ambience of a room. Please do not forget this in the dining room. Soft lighting can truly enhance the enjoyment of a meal.*

This client loves to entertain and isn't afraid of bold statements. The wallpaper by Sanderson could seem like a fussy choice, but when combined with contemporary elements, it really is the star of the show.

A farmhouse dining table paired with modern chairs? Why not?

The first selection for this dining room was the set of vintage Hans Wegner chairs from an antique dealer in Denmark. The large-scale photograph of the California coast by Emily Johnson provides a dramatic backdrop.

right: This tabletop is composed of synthetic quartz that resembles marble, but is more durable. It withstands the inevitable red wine spills at MacRostie Winery.

opposite: These vintage chairs were found online and recovered in a multicolored woven wool fabric. A fabric with pattern or movement is ideal for disguising potential stains.

## CONSIDER YOUR OPTIONS

Since dining rooms are typically underutilized and are predominantly reserved for special occasions, consider alternative options for this space, such as lining a wall with bookcases to create a library-like feel. The dining room table can make a great space to use as an office. Much of this book was written sitting at the dining room table with my laptop, with photos and concepts spread across the surface. (Copious amounts of coffee and wine were involved as well.)

The dining room is the heart of the home for this large family, who constantly hosts events and family gatherings. The table is meant for the outdoors, but why not break some rules? If you can't decide on one style of seating, mix a few different styles with some commonality (such as the tone of wood).

opposite: The Saarinen table is a favorite of mine, and I've used it in a number of projects. Here, the iconic piece is coupled with French bistro chairs made of woven plastic that make them easy to keep clean. Instead of just hanging one light fixture above a table, consider a pair to enhance the interest.

left: Don't forget about the backs of chairs. This is a great chance to incorporate an additional textile into a space. The print by John Robshaw adds whimsy to this client's breakfast room.

## GET CREATIVE

In my experience, the dining room is the least used room in most homes. Most people use the space for more formal gatherings or holidays. The cost of a dozen chairs and a table can be quite high, but you can get creative if you're on a budget. For many years, I used an inexpensive folding plywood table and covered it with a simple tablecloth. This worked until I was able to find the right table, and the temporary solution gave me time to save for this larger purchase. I am also a huge fan of more casual dining, and I personally favor a plate on my lap in my living room—a great solution for anyone who doesn't have the formal dining space! (Just make sure you have plenty of napkins handy.)

above: A trip to Portugal was breathtaking, with blue-and-white tile work around every corner. When traveling, think about how you can adapt concepts from memorable sights to your own interior.

right: This is a favorite dining room that I designed for the San Francisco Decorator Showcase house. I was looking to mix some unexpected pieces together. I went bold with bright green leather Louis XVI chairs and antique Chinese pottery. The branching light fixture from Lindsey Adelman virtually floats above the table.

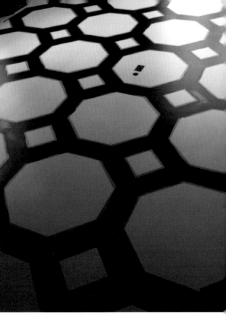

## KNOW YOUR LIFESTYLE

When it comes to surfaces, glass tables can be a nightmare for some, as people fear they will always need to be cleaned. I have had a glass top now for years and I love the durability. Overly precious antique tables can cause you to gasp at dinners at the sight of a drop of water. Before committing to a table, figure out what will work for your lifestyle. A good option with young children (or messy adults) is a table with natural imperfections or patina, such as a farmhouse table. Ring marks blend in and can even add to the charm.

opposite: The banquette fabric by Raoul served as the starting point for this breakfast room. I had the linen laminated with a matte coating, which renders it nearly indestructible to the two young boys who live in the house. We selected the perfect shade of blue grosgrain ribbon to trim the white linen roman shades, drawing the palette from the banquette fabric.

left: This dining room table was found at a flea market in Paris. It didn't come with a top, so I had a thick piece of glass created for it. It was important that the tabletop be clear to showcase the geometric design of the table base.

opposite: Seagrass area rugs serve as a neutral base. The Greek key detail lends visual interest. The client already owned these beautiful blue dining chairs, which provided a great launching point for the design.

Fiddle leaf trees are very popular, and it's easy to understand why: They add great color and height to a room. If you have trouble keeping greenery alive, there are some very realistic faux options on the market.

above: Pro tip for selecting paints and fabrics: Start with your fabrics, and then move on to your paints. It is simple enough to adjust your paint colors, while fabric options can be more limited.

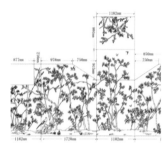

above: Viewing a mock-up of a wallpaper is a great way to visualize its ultimate appearance in a space. It is extremely helpful when the wallpaper vendor can provide a layout. De Gournay and Gracie are two significant producers who offer Chinoiserie patterns. The color and pattern options are limitless.

right: Think about the transition from room to room. This foyer has a geometric wallpaper that flows into the dining room, where the pattern is more organic.

opposite: I was a little nervous showing this client lavender leather for dining room chairs, but I am glad that I took that chance. The unexpected color really makes a statement.

overlay: In this loft-like apartment that lacks predefined zones, the light fixture is a statement piece that defines the formal dining area.

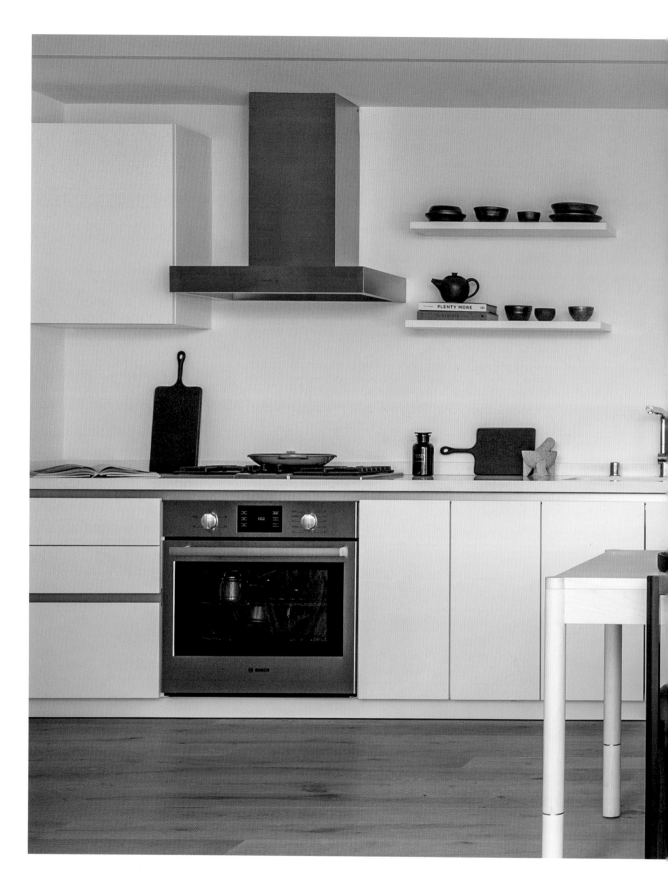

# Kitchens

It's absolutely true what they say about a kitchen—it's the heart and soul of a home. I tend toward classic foundations, which may be layered with personal accents. I am always seeking a balance when designing a space, no matter the room.

At our first meeting, this client had stacks of kitchen images from Italy and Spain that featured old tiled floors. I knew immediately that a statement floor had to be incorporated into this project.

above: We channeled the colors of the Atelier Brancusi in Paris for the floor and painted cabinets in this kitchen. We were even able to incorporate a touch of gold in the form of the brass faucet.

Whenever you can request samples from a vendor, take the time and effort to do so. Be cognizant that the appearance of a product on your computer screen may be very different from its appearance in person.

right: The chair in this kitchen allows for a spot to leaf through cookbooks.

opposite: When a kitchen is very long and lacks a center island, planning out the positions of appliances and workspaces is critical. These pendant lights are from a salvage yard in Portland, Oregon.

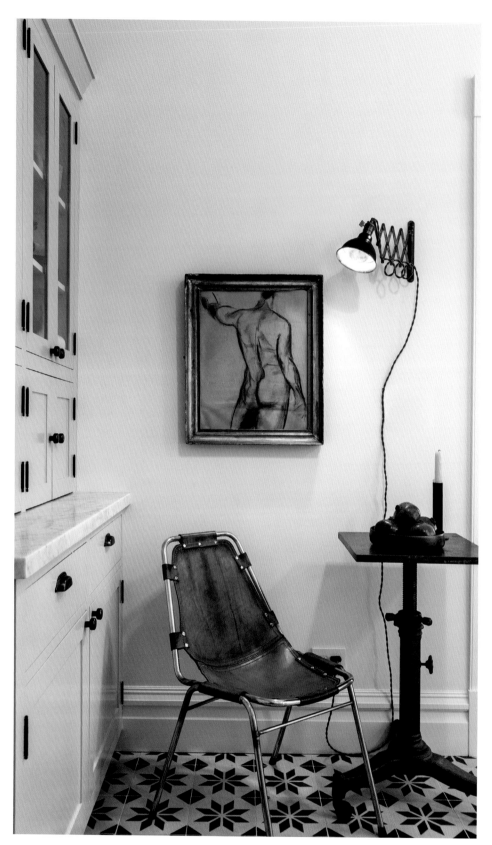

## START WITH ESSENTIALS

In conceptualizing a kitchen, I think of the layout in terms of a triangle that forms the joinder of the three most critical kitchen appliances: the refrigerator, the range, and the sink. Everything else is built around the seamless integration of these essentials. A kitchen can't just be pretty; it has to be functional. Consider adding the aesthetic touches as a reward for accomplishing this utilitarian task. I prefer to design spaces that I describe as timeless: spaces that will not begin to look dated with the arrival of a new design trend. You can always alter accessories or repaint to keep a space au courant; but by selecting classic elements, you will create a space that will stand the test of time.

above: When embarking on a new project, Pinterest and Instagram are great sources to search for ideas. I am still a bit old-fashioned, however; I like to visualize things in print.

right: This copper hood was left over from the previous kitchen design. It was the only item we maintained. I love that it adds a different metal to the room that is a departure from commonly used stainless steel. Don't shy away from mixing metals—it adds visual interest.

left: This client is a frequent traveler, but when at home, spends most of the time in the kitchen. Stainless steel is an underutilized material for countertops. It is affordable, easy to clean, and has been used in commercial kitchens for years.

above: If you have the space and budget, a pair of ovens is the way to go. Since I'm tall, I like that this configuration elevates the placement of the ovens. It makes for easier use than an oven below a range top.

## CHOOSE YOUR STATEMENT PIECE

Unquestionably, the marble is the star of the show in this kitchen. The natural beauty of the white and gray veins immediately draws the eye upon entering. Think about such things when designing a space. Which element do you want to make the biggest statement? It is extremely helpful to build a room around a statement piece. Is it the marble on the counters, the area rug in your living room, or that graphic wallpaper that you want to use in your guest room? Think about it like you do when you get dressed each morning. Coco Chanel once said, "Before leaving the house, a lady should look in the mirror and remove one accessory." I carry this advice into decorating. Select your bold statement and then build around it with neutrals or complementary accents. This will maintain the elegance over time.

The brass hood and solid marble backsplash in this kitchen are striking. We could have selected black or gray cabinets, but felt a rich navy blue was fresh. Notice that the countertops are not the same material as the backsplash; they are a man-made quartz. It would have been overly busy if the counters were the same material—plus, the synthetic quartz is much more affordable.

Because there are so many elements involved in designing and decorating a kitchen, the following are some questions to mull over, suggestions, and tips to help you plan your design.

## STORAGE

How do you purchase food for your family? Do you make daily trips to the market, or, do larger weekly hauls? Where is everything going to go?

Do you need to consider an extra freezer or refrigerator? Do you have room for this in the kitchen, pantry, or garage?

If you cook often, think about organizing based on how frequently you use certain items and place them accordingly.

The locations of the trash can, compost bin, and recycling receptacle should be planned out at the beginning, not added in as an afterthought. Think about accessibility. Compost, for example, is mandatory in San Francisco. In my next kitchen design, I might consider a cutout in the countertop that allows for items to go down a shoot, directly into the trash can, instead of always having to open a cabinet door.

If you do not have the space for a pantry (which I personally do not), think about another option in the room that could work for items not used daily. I added a bookcase along an unused wall that helps accommodate pantry items.

The storage in this kitchen is intentionally directed away from the kitchen, so that the many members of this busy family can access the dishes without interfering with the cooking process. The industrial refrigerator ideally suits this family of six, who frequently host other family and friends.

above top: Open shelves are an excellent way to display collections. The black pottery assemblage is comprised of pieces I made, so they have a special significance to me.

above bottom: I wasn't able to find the precise tile size I desired for my kitchen, so I had my contractor cut 24-inch-by-24-inch pieces of stone and lay them in a herringbone pattern.

right: Subway tiles are always in style and usually well-priced. In this case, I opted to take the tiles to the ceiling, which make cleaning up kitchen splashes very easy.

opposite: Installing the La Cornue Château series range was a dream come true. I love how the black enamel finish pairs with the lower cabinets.

## APPLIANCES

Do you prefer a gas or electric range? What about a convection versus conventional oven? Do your research online and in-person at appliance stores. Ask your friends what they do and do not like about their own selections. I have some very specific feelings about certain brands and, unfortunately, have had to learn from my own trial and error. Fortunately, I can pass my insights on to my clients when they are making these decisions.

Do you use a microwave, toaster oven, or coffee maker? Do you want them out on the counter full time?

Do you have a plan to disguise or hide small appliances so they do not always end up out on the counters? In my opinion, things like large mixers and blenders should be stored in cabinets for their infrequent use. Clearly, modify that suggestion if you make daily smoothies or are a baker. Make sure to review all specifications that require plumbing or special power sources.

Do you have a large family or entertain in a way that requires multiple ovens or dishwashers?

Many of my clients collect wine and may have wine cellars, but they enjoy having a few bottles more accessible for day-to-day use. A small wine fridge can be useful in such cases.

If you have kids, do you want to create a separate drawer for snacks? This is a great way to have a self-service spot for kids or hungry spouses. I don't have kids, but I do have a snack drawer with easy access to trail mix, chocolates, popcorn, and pretzels.

## SINKS

When thinking about the sink, there are numerous options, including porcelain, farmhouse style, and stainless steel. Do you need an additional sink of a certain depth for washing large pots and pans? In my kitchen, I decided that I wanted to create the sink out of marble, and I had it fabricated with the same slabs as the countertops. Also, I have yet to meet a drying rack that is attractive, so I had grooves cut into the marble to allow for drainage right into the sink. It was one of the best decisions I made in my own home remodel.

Do you like the idea of a built-in soap dispenser? A nice detail can be a decorative bowl—perhaps a travel souvenir—for sponges, or a decorative bottle for scented dish soap to make washing up a more pleasant experience.

opposite: My sink was created out of the same marble as the countertops. I always dreamed of creating something like this for its uniqueness. It genuinely adds enjoyment while washing dishes.

left: Sink stations are not always for washing dishes. A farmhouse style offers extra depth and square footage for flower arranging or even washing a dog.

*There is this misconception that marble is precious, and that it is easily stained and etched. Properly treated, marble countertops will last a lifetime. Remember: Marble has been used in France and Italy for centuries. Enough said.*

above: The sprayer is always a useful tool. The integration of this sprayer into the faucet achieves a modern elegance.

right: The Cherner bar stools in walnut infuse a modern element into this classic kitchen. The marble counters and white cabinetry keep the kitchen feeling timeless and bright.

opposite: It might look like each of these cabinets are the same white hue, but they are actually varying shades. By using samples, you can pair the cabinet color to the actual stone selection. We had the cabinet maker paint samples on the doors and took them with us to the marble yard when making our final selection for countertops.

left: The Hicks pendant lights are among my favorites to use in a kitchen project. Good lighting is essential, as is a designated spot for your cookbooks (such as the end of an island for easy access).

above: If you have the space, an extra sink is a luxury. You can use it for prep work, handwashing, or clean up.

## OPEN SHELVING

Do you like things to appear to be clean and orderly? Open shelves and glass cabinets can layer an interesting element and break up the visual wall of cabinets. But don't overdo it. Displaying all your treasured wedding china may simply look cluttered, and it can be hard to keep objects looking perfectly arranged all the time.

below: Open shelves provide useful space to display a few of your favorite cookbooks. I also like to create small vignettes of flowers or meaningful objects.

right: Rather than closing off the side of a kitchen island, consider open shelving to enhance storage capacity.

right: Large refrigeration units in stainless steel can sometimes overpower a space. By paneling the refrigerator, less attention is drawn to its size.

opposite: Glass cabinets allow you to display beautiful objects. But be careful not to overdo the amount of glass cabinets in a kitchen; chances are that not everything you own is visually pleasing.

Roman shades provide an opportunity to add pattern and color to a kitchen. Here, we chose a Quadrille ikat fabric that adds a touch of softness.

opposite: California's indoor/outdoor lifestyle is ideal for these clients. Fresh flowers, fruit, and vegetables from their garden are always in abundance. I have been lucky enough to receive fresh goodies to take home with me.

left: Adding modern artwork keeps this breakfast room feeling fresh. The Quadrille fabric on the chairs was laminated to protect from the wear and tear of four children.

## FINAL CONSIDERATIONS

If you have children, do you want to create an area to keep an eye on them while you are prepping? Do you want a central place for children to do homework, or simply be with you, while you are working in the kitchen? Or, are you able to designate a corner of the island for them to help with the work?

On this note, can you tolerate guests in your kitchen while you are cooking? Or, do you prefer to be secluded? I prefer the latter, and I find the preparation experience to be relaxing, creative, and personal. I really don't want people hovering around me.

There is a trend toward the open floor plan. If you'd rather not look at a sink full of dishes while eating dinner, it may be wise to choose a design that separates your kitchen from your dining area.

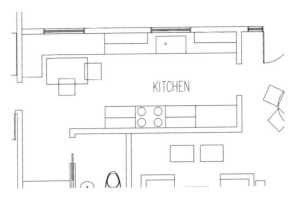

left: This kitchen opens to both the breakfast room and the living room, so the client can keep an eye on the kids. The barstools add an industrial layer to the kitchen, which is a nice counterbalance to an otherwise traditional scheme.

above: Tile in pale blue imparts a reflective quality. The tiles are handmade, resulting in a slightly different shade of blue on each one.

overlay: The understated color scheme in this kitchen is intended to draw the eye to the magnificent exterior garden.

opposite: If this were my kitchen, I would find it really difficult to accomplish anything because I would be constantly gazing out at the garden. I love the detail of the wall of windows.

left: Don't forget about the ceilings or the sides of cabinets. Why not add an architectural element?

above: Prep areas are must-haves in kitchen design—from places to wash fresh produce, to surfaces that work well for chopping. I like to have extra cutting boards tucked away—yet easily within reach—to keep countertops looking their best.

right: This banquette was designed with pull-out drawers under the seating, which increases the functionality of this design. The drawers are filled with everything from crayons to place mats—all accessible, yet easy to put away when not in use.

right: If your kitchen is large enough to have a separate butler's pantry, this is a great area for storing fancy glassware and favorite liquors. The copper cups for Moscow Mules might not be used every day, but are fun to bring out for parties and special events.

opposite: With everyone on the go and running around these days, it is nice to take some time to enjoy breakfast together on weekends. Adding a beach photo that reminds you of a vacation can further put you in a leisurely, relaxed state.

# Bedrooms

Rooms should always feel welcoming. This, of course, applies to the bedroom as well. This is a space that should feel comfortable and inviting—somewhere to escape the world and recharge. After all, most of us spend about a third of our lives in our bedrooms. My king-sized bed is one of my favorite places; it provides sanctuary from my daily stresses. It is dressed in a mix of bedding, from IKEA sheets to mono-grammed linens by Matouk. Can we be really honest? I know many of you make your bed daily. I am not one of you. Sorry to ruin the vision that you might have had of me.

A dealer in Germany had a pair of these vintage George Nelson bedside tables, and we knew we had to have them for this bedroom. The area rug and grass cloth add texture and tie together the shades of blue. The mounted sconces are a perfect understated accent.

## SELECT THE RIGHT BED

I am not going to sugarcoat it: selecting a bed can be a challenge. I've seen plenty of couples, who otherwise rarely seem to disagree, have prolonged arguments about this! Why? Well, for starters, there are so many options, from platforms that are low to the ground for those who like a modern look, to canopy beds in wood or metal. For comfort, I am a big fan of upholstered headboards. And, since the fabric choices are pretty much unlimited, you can make these work in any setting. If you start with a neutral foundation, add patterns and textures to create visual interest. I lean toward solids since they tend to hold up over time without feeling dated. But if you feel like your aesthetic changes every few years, or want to experiment with a statement fabric, go for it—it's easy enough to have the headboard recovered later. Don't forget to think about the size and scale of a bed. Take into account ceiling heights for a canopy bed, or how a sleigh bed's curves may occupy a lot of visual space.

opposite: Wesley typically sleeps in his own bed, so it was a bit of an indulgence for him to sit atop the bed in this photograph. I love how he matches the crisp black-and-white of the bedding.

above: An accent of black is timeless. Since it anchors the bedroom, we selected it for this clean-lined canopy bed. The scalloped bedding and monogrammed pillows make getting into bed at the end of the day a special treat.

## THROW OUT THE RULES

Bedside tables are one area where I think all of the rules can go out the window. Who really made up these rules anyway? Bedside tables do not need to match. They can be large, or small if you do not have very much room. I have used dressers as bedside tables as well as desks. My side of the bed has a 20-inch round table with a lamp on top. I have stacks of books and magazines, as well as the dog bed just below. You can also find my ear plugs, eye mask, lip balm, notepad and pen (for those brilliant ideas in the middle of the night), and multiple drinking vessels. Again, sorry to tarnish the preconceived notions that you had of me. In my perfect world, my own home would be as orderly as the photos in this book.

opposite left: A bed cover can be used to enhance the color of a bedroom. In particular, it is a great opportunity to incorporate a textile discovered on a favorite travel experience.

opposite right: We designed this custom headboard with built-in padding for comfortable bedtime reading. The intensity of the green is the focal point, so the surrounding furnishings are all neutrals.

above: This burled nightstand is low enough to place stacks of books, or for easy access to a glass of water in the middle of the night. Leaning art from a flea market gives it a relaxed feeling—·and requires a lot less work and commitment than hanging!

opposite: This room was designed for a client's daughter, who was away at college at the time. We wanted the room to reflect her favorite color—purple—but also work for other houseguests.

left: This client wanted a monochromatic bedroom that would be a peaceful sanctuary at the end of the day. We had the bedside tables custom-made because there wasn't much room next to the closet door. We added vintage hardware for a unique touch. Swing arm reading lamps are functional and offer the ultimate in flexibility.

## BRING TOGETHER TEXTILES

At the end of a long day—ok, even a leisurely day—I love collapsing on a bed
dressed in several layers of bedding. A soft
pile of linens is such a luxury, yet also so
simple to achieve. You can keep it classic
with all white sheets, duvet covers, quilts,
or blankets, but add interest by varying the
fabrics and trims (plain and textured cot-
ton, lace, embroidery). Or you can bring
together a mélange of styles for a look
that's more bohemian. When mixing patterns, it's important to keep the scale and
colors of each print in mind so you don't
end up with a circus effect. And, when
making your textile decisions, don't forget
the window treatments, which, in addition
to being functional, provide a finished feeling to a room. Roman shades are ideal if
you want a clean-lined appearance, while
curtains—depending on how full and long
they are, and the choice of fabric—can be
contemporary or over-the-top luxurious.
No matter which type of treatment best
suits a space, I usually opt for a blackout
lining for extra darkness.

Don't shy away from mixing patterns. In this
bedroom suite, I mixed ikat, animal print, and a
marbled Christopher Spitzmiller lamp.

above and opposite: The arches in Jaipur, India, inspired us to use this Galbraith & Paul wallpaper as the backdrop for a bedroom. Pillows in marigold worked as a perfect accent to brighten up the space.

right: This bedroom's soothing tones are reminiscent of beaches and sea glass. The glass lamp blends into the interior, rather than detracting from other key elements like the textiles and artwork.

This client wanted to create comfortable suite-like quarters for his mother's frequent visits. The room was large enough to fit a queen-size bed alongside chairs and a large ottoman. It is a perfect spot to curl up by the fire and enjoy a book after a long plane ride.

## MAKE GUESTS FEEL AT HOME

Like your own bedroom, guest rooms should be inviting and comforting. Think about all the amenities that impress you when you check into a great hotel or B&B: fresh linens, extra pillows, a new bar of soap, a spot for suitcases, drawers and hanging closet space. Going the extra mile with touches like a candle, flowers, and a carafe of water are always thoughtful. Adequate lighting is also key, as are accessible plugs for charging phones and computers. If you want to give it a test run, spend the night in your own guest room and think about the comforts that could improve your guest's experience.

I like to create vignettes on bedside tables—filled with favorite objects, flowers, and books—to personalize a space. These are easily changed, so take a risk if a design trend strikes your fancy. You can easily change it later, when it becomes passé.

Tucked into the corner of a bedroom, this tulip chair in green is the perfect perch for looking out onto the city. (The grouping of art by Josef Albers isn't so bad to look at either.)

opposite: As you can probably guess, the concrete column in this bedroom made furniture placement a challenge. Thankfully, this blue dresser fits snugly in the spot and, with a pair of abstract paintings by William McLure in the style of Cy Twombly, we created a lovely design moment.

above: Wouldn't you like to wake up to this view? This is a bedroom in the private residence at Nine Suns Winery in Napa. Their branding color is orange, so I thought this canopy bed would be fun.

Collections need to be grouped, with negative space around them. This allows for breathing room and for the pieces to be highlighted. It is called a collection, not clutter. Even the most mundane items can be interesting if displayed well. Collections can be a bowl full of stones or shells that you have picked up at the beach, mismatched candlesticks, or a stack of books by your favorite authors.

opposite: A bookcase doesn't have to be filled with books running in the same direction. We grouped these to form small collections. The vase and flowers break up the linear look of the shelves and books.

left: Who says a bookcase needs to be boring? We had this bookcase made in a green color with a treatment that really shows off the grain of the oak. And I love the way the television blends into the bookcase; you hardly know it's there.

above: Here I chose accessories that matched the colors of the book covers—white, cream, and black—for a dramatic effect. The middle shelf, made up of mostly white and cream hues, allows the eye a place to rest.

opposite: We wanted art that would bring together the colors in this bedroom, so we commissioned this piece by Brian Coleman. The rigid lines of the light fixture are offset by the fluidity of the abstract painting.

# Kids' Rooms

Kids' rooms evolve more quickly than any other room in the house. From what I've been told, in a heartbeat you'll be moving from cribs and changing tables to toddler beds, elementary age to high school, and then, if you are lucky enough, a room for your grown children to come home to. Therefore, I suggest that these rooms not be decorated impulsively. If there is a theme to these tips, it would be flexibility. And just think: If you are not redecorating from scratch at every stage, it will allow for more money into their college funds.

This is one of my all-time favorite rooms for twins. I love how the map mural sets the tone for the rest of the choices in the space. The wooden white beds are from Pottery Barn Kids, which will last for years to come. The monogrammed letter pillows are from Etsy, while the black-and-white striped rug is IKEA. (I know parents don't always want to break the bank for kids' rooms!)

## ANTICIPATE TRANSITION

Think about the sweet wallpaper with the ABCs or animals and the overall life that it will have. When will you or your child grow tired of this? Consider that childish motifs will not last into adolescence. I am not advising that you create boring spaces. You can accessorize a room with age-appropriate accents that can be gradually replaced over time. My approach emphasizes décor that will provide future flexibility. A space does not have to be designed to reflect gender. "Musical bedrooms" tends to happen with the announcement of a new addition: One child is shifted to another room to accommodate the new arrival. Fortunately, accents and trims can easily be changed. When neutral backgrounds are the backdrop, these rooms can transition with less hassle.

opposite: In this nursery, instead of purchasing a separate changing table, I incorporated it onto the dresser. This avoids the need for a subsequent redesign as the table is easily removed. Wallpaper is always a fun way to inject whimsy into a child's room.

above: At first, gray walls might seem too dark for a kid's room, but when contrasted with a playful, green dresser, it absolutely works. The framed shadow box of Boy Scout badges belonged to the client's father.

right: Miffy the rabbit actually illuminates, functioning as a fun night-light. Notice that the yellow Campaign dressers are actually two pushed together to appear as one large piece. If you can't find what you are looking for, make modifications to suit your space.

opposite: The Kelly Wearstler wallpaper adds an unexpected abstract element to this room. The modern bed is not overly fussy. Trundles are a godsend for slumber parties.

## TONE IT DOWN

Our clients' children are often very outspoken. While they may be insistent on a particular favorite color, I've learned over the years that favorites change—sometimes even daily. Try to tone down the current favorites with colors that might not tire as easily, creating rooms that will have longer lives. Kids are notorious for changing their personal tastes frequently. This is all part of growing up and developing their style and personality. But it can be expensive and time-consuming to update their room décor constantly.

*I am often asked about my favorite room to design. Kids' rooms might top the list. I am not sure if it is a chance for me to relive my own youth or the idea of being able to collaborate with a child to discover his or her budding tastes and styles. And maybe influence them a little?*

opposite: The headboard and fabric—Brunschwig & Fils' Les Touches—served as the starting point for this tween's bedroom.

above: The boat bed was a hand-me-down from this boy's older brother. The blue-and-white striped bedding and Greek key trim on the window shades deliver graphic punches.

## PICK A THEME

Although I always like to consider how a child's room will evolve, there are times when the client is all-in on a theme and makes a conscious decision to worry about future iterations of the room, well, in the future. I won't lie: For a designer, this can be a lot of fun. Especially once the finished room is revealed to the kids.

As little ones develop into big kids, they desire a more grown-up look. One way to give them what they want without losing the youthful feel is to capitalize on their favorite activities. Beyond just featuring a sports team or favorite boy band, which may be a passing craze, the idea is to reinforce an enduring talent or hobby. Wallpapers can be a fun way to really go all out. For this project, the son loved baseball, so we blew up a favorite photo to create wallpaper for the entire back wall. We went bold with this idea. Because a certain sports team may be a passing craze, we opted for an overall theme rather than something too specific. We also did this with a twins' bedroom with a large-scale map. It was a bold choice and has had several varied arrangements over the years.

Although baseball is certainly the overarching theme of this boy's room, we decided against utilizing the colors of his favorite team. Instead, we opted for a neutral black-and-white image that allowed for versatility in selecting the furnishings.

right: The end result belies the simplicity of this wall treatment: We taped out the pattern to create a modern take on mountains. It's a neutral backdrop for whatever the occupant's current obsession. (For now, it's Star Wars—hence the bedding.)

opposite: We even design rooms for non-human children. "Best in Show" wallpaper by Thibaut and a black-and-white checkered tile floor was the perfect choice for this client's beloved pup.

# Powder Rooms and Bathrooms

Designers often liken powder rooms to jewel boxes. Their compact size encourages more risks and playfulness than, say, an expansive master bath. With powder rooms, you can break the rules, since the space doesn't necessarily have to relate to any of the other interiors in the house. Go bold with wallpaper or a paint treatment. The details—guest towels, nice soap, and fresh flowers (a small room means you can get away with just a single stem in a bud vase)—can inject personality.

Since we went bold with the wallpaper by MAKELIKE, we kept it simple with the mirror. If the client ever decides to change out those elements, the marble countertop and subway tiles are classic, and will work well with practically anything.

opposite: The black-and-white wallpaper from Quadrille in this powder room allows the brass of the washstand to pop.

left: This Scalamandre zebra wallpaper is a favorite—I have used it in every available color. In this instance, it makes bath time extra fun.

## MAKE A STATEMENT

Wallpaper has made a major comeback, and I think it is here to stay. Rooms that are well ventilated or void of a lot of moisture are generally good candidates, so a powder room can be an ideal place to transform with wallpaper. Why not try a large-scale or busy pattern? Think of this space as your chance to make a statement.

I had wanted to use this Katie Ridder wallpaper for years. I finally found a home for it in this bathroom.

The iconic Fireworks by Albert Hadley wallpaper sparkles in this monochromatic bathroom.
We even wrapped the sconce lampshades in some of the leftover wallpaper. Edging the roman
shades, the grosgrain ribbon in a Greek key detail echoes the back lacquered mirror.

Since blue and white was this client's favorite color combination, there was no doubt about the palette for the wallpaper in the powder room of this 1906 house. (Yes, those are original molding details.) We layered an antique gold mirror, sconces from Paris, and monogrammed hand towels for a personal touch.

above: Sanderson wallpaper brings this kids' bathroom to life. The vanity in powder-coated metal reminds me of elementary school lockers—and I like that the cabinet is off the ground, so it's easy to mop up after bath time.

opposite: Abnormals Anonymous' Bruce wallpaper, with its whale bone motif, was chosen for two boys who share this bathroom. Dual sinks were critical to avoid a line for teeth-brushing time! We had the vanity base made with a shelf that can hold baskets or extra rolls of toilet paper.

The hexagon is a classic tile pattern, but in this bathroom it is made modern with large black tiles. We had the floating vanity and open shelves constructed from wood for an organic touch.

## USE LAYERS AND DETAILS

Just like every other room in the house, bathrooms need to be thought-out. Unless the look you are after is a sterile hygienic lab (which is a preference for some), think of the ways you can add decorating details and layers to the functionality and efficiency of the space. How do you do this? Let's start with the fallacy that you need a medicine cabinet. Consider an alternative storage solution and swap out the mirror with something that offers some interest. This really breaks up the hard surfaces and is a bit unexpected.

You may want to tone down the use of antique glass mirrors in your everyday bathroom. At times it is nice not to notice every line and wrinkle, but in the case of your usual bathroom, you do want to actually see yourself. And can we all agree that those magnifying mirrors should be kept in a drawer? Personally, I don't need any more of a fright first thing in the morning with my bedhead. I prefer natural light in bathrooms, but realize that is not always possible. Don't forget about layering lighting in the bathroom and adding dimmers.

above left: Design public service announcement: You don't have to stick with metal tones for your bathroom fixtures. Have fun with color. These orange powder coated fixtures are a delightful surprise when you enter the room.

above right: Moroccan-inspired tiles inset in this shower hit just the right note: It might have been overpowering to do the entire shower in this color or pattern. A little can go a long way.

opposite: Sconces are typical in bathrooms, but in a tight area like this we didn't want to sacrifice precious wall space. The large-scale mirror gives the illusion of a bigger room. We opted for an asymmetrical cluster of glass orbs for a different twist.

opposite: We went all-in on marble tile here, with a floor-to-ceiling installation—and even wrapping the tub in the tile. The white garden stool is a great spot to put your towel before a long soak in the tub.

left: The brass hardware on the vanity was added to create the look of a piece of Campaign-style furniture.

## THROW IN THE TOWEL

For hardware, I prefer hooks over towel bars. They are more relaxed and create added visual interest. There's a school of thought that towels never seem to dry completely this way. I don't have this problem, and I doubt you will either. I love how towels can make a space feel a little bit more individualized. You can choose colors, trims, or monograms, if that is your thing. (I may have once filled an entire suitcase with towels from Istanbul.) However, you should have a special towel—a hand towel—that you put out just for guests.

If you do not have a window in a bathroom and are on the top floor, consider a skylight to allow natural light into a space. To make the case for doing so, I often show my clients this photo I took during a trip to Sicily, showing domed skylights. The effect is beautiful and dramatic, and the image really helps illustrate the concept.

right: When it comes to showers, your options are pretty much a glass shower door or a curtain. Or are they? I really love the look of old steel case windows. After having no luck searching for an old window large enough to use for a shower, I had this panel fabricated for my bathroom.

opposite: Floor-to-ceiling subway tile is a great choice for a wet room like a bathroom. A bonus for me is that I can easily shower my pup without worrying about the mess. I brought the striped towel pictured here back from Istanbul several years ago.

opposite: Three teenage boys share this bathroom. We didn't want to make it too childlike, or too mature. The saturation of the green subway tile keeps the space fresh and fun.

left: As you can now see, I use subway tiles quite a bit in bathrooms. If you want to change up the look, try a different color grout. Here, a black grout completely alters the look. The green and blue floor tiles enliven an otherwise neutral color scheme.

## ACCESSORIZE

As for other accessories in a bathroom, I try to avoid the standard toothbrush holder and soap dish. In your travels, look for a vessel such as a cup holder or small vase that can add to the layering and personalization. Plus, it will be a lovely reminder of a favorite vacation. Baskets make for a great textural element that's also functional; use them to store extra towels (rolled up), as a more attractive waste basket (no plastic trash cans, please), or to hold abundant rolls of toilet paper.

opposite: Powder rooms are great for pedestal sinks, where concealed storage isn't usually such a priority. The open space beneath the sink is well spent on an attractive basket filled with rolls of toilet paper, so your guests can easily spot them.

above left: During my travels, I've come across plenty of items that I wanted to bring home. Acting on this impulse would require me to rent a warehouse just to store them. As I've noted, consider something small—because when it comes to evoking memories of a special trip, size doesn't necessarily matter. Something as simple as a small vase is enough.

above right: There are no rules when it comes to lighting. These sconces are typically found in a library, but there's no reason they can't work in a bathroom equally well. Note that the sconce is brass and the fixtures and hardware are polished nickel—proof that you can harmoniously mix metals.

above: This client is an avid yogi, so having a steam shower that opens to an outdoor patio—where the client engages in morning yoga stretches—is ideal.

right: Most of us have a lot of products, and leaving them spread over the counter isn't preferable. If you have your medicine cabinet recessed into the wall, it will simply appear to be a vanity mirror.

right: The simplicity of a neutral bathroom allows for the faucets to become the focal point—like pieces of jewelry.

opposite: I love supporting artists and allowing them to be creative, so decorative painter Katherine Jacobus had free rein in this powder room. We simply asked her to create something unique and eye-catching. Mission accomplished.

Clients often tell us that they want their bathrooms to feel like a day spa. We can't blame them—and in this large space, we achieved that goal by installing an oversized soaking tub and a skylight over the shower.

## EMBRACE ART

Art is something people often don't think about for the bathroom. But this can be the perfect place for snapshots of loved ones or postcards of favorite destinations. I keep a collection of love notes and funny *New Yorker* cartoons on the inside door of the medicine cabinet. And yes, I did just say medicine cabinet after clearly telling you that you don't need one. To each his own.

opposite: Don't overlook art in your bathrooms. Framed antique architectural prints add another layer of sophistication to this project. To avoid potential damage to art, keep in mind that well-ventilated spaces are best in order to keep the moisture out.

left: This Cole & Sons Fornasetti Malachite wallpaper proves that you can add drama without color—you just need an amazing pattern!

Pretty in pink, indeed! This master bathroom was kissed by the softest rosy walls. The hardware is a combination of brass with Lucite, and the pink towels are a welcome change from the usual white.

This is a master bathroom that I designed for the San Francisco Decorator Showcase house. Unexpected elements such as the gilt mirror and antique marble silhouettes from Rome imbue warmth in a space that might feel cold with marble and other hard materials.

# Finishing Touches

So you've made all of the big decisions—paint, tile, furniture, flooring. The details are what can make a room go from good to great. Collected treasures, art, and books help define ourselves through our spaces.

## EVOLUTION

I think of my own home as a laboratory, and I am constantly making changes. With this mindset, I'm more inclined to take risks—and this is something I usually stress with my clients. If you have a large collection, not everything has to be on display at the same time. Try out various pieces in the collection and rotate things in and out depending on your mood. Set aside space in a closet, garage, or storage unit for any overflow items.

## LIGHTING

When designers talk about layered lighting, what they're referring to is lighting from a range of sources—overhead, sconces, table lamps. I talked about lighting in the Primer chapter, but I am mentioning it again here because it is something that can continue to evolve. Not only does lighting provide a chance to infuse some personality into a space, but it serves different purposes when you're spending time in a room. Ambient light—such as recessed lighting, flush or semi-flush mount fixtures, and ceiling fans with lights—provides general illumination, and is the most important layer. It's being able to flip on a light switch and see the surroundings. Task lighting is utilitarian and more specific to an activity, like a reading spot or a bathroom vanity. Accent lighting dresses up a room; think of it as jewelry for a space. For example, a pretty lamp may not give off the most light, but it adds visual interest.

## ART

Art can really add to the personality of your home. And never, ever think that you can't afford art! With eBay, Etsy, flea markets, and garage sales, art has become increasingly accessible. And then, of course, there are the galleries out there—offline and online—that are excellent sources. No matter your budget, there's no reason to live with bare walls, unless, of course, you want to. Some of my favorite art displays in clients' homes have cost very little. Grouping artwork in a gallery-style enhances the overall effect by mixing an array of images in different sizes and shapes. A painting from a flea market, a child's sketch, and a photo from your recent vacation can all live together in harmony. (Yes, even kids' art or personal photography takes on a level of importance when framed and arranged on a wall.) Include one larger piece that will serve as an anchor for the smaller surrounding items. You may want to do a "test drive" by laying out the arrangement on the floor to aid your visualization. It is important to be patient as you curate your gallery wall. This is not about throwing random pieces together and hoping for the best.

opposite: A beautiful sunny afternoon in the tasting room at MacRostie Winery. I commissioned these paintings by Robert Roth.

above top: Discovering objects in Mexico City.

above middle: Example of a personalized gallery.

above bottom: Shopping for textiles in Istanbul.

*If you are not a frequent traveler, you can recreate this look and concept with many options at flea markets or online stores that specialize in far flung objects. Handcrafted textiles add a layer of richness and texture, and can bring a unique worldliness to your home.*

## FLOWERS AND PLANTS

It's amazing what a difference a handful of fresh blooms can make! And no, you don't have to hit up the fancy florist every week. People are often intimidated by flowers because they are unsure precisely how to put together an arrangement. Grab a few options at your local grocery store or garden center. Greenery adds visual interest and texture to a space. If you want something low maintenance, succulents and cactus are the way to go. They add a living, green element that requires little investment—money- or time-wise. Don't be afraid to ask the sales associates at your local nursery a lot of questions to determine which plants will survive best in your home. Interestingly, orchids are not only beautiful but they are low maintenance: they can last for months and don't require a green thumb. Indoor trees create height in a space. Consider faux plants as a fool-proof option.

## TEXTILES

As previously touched upon, gathering textiles while on a trip is another way to bring back a memory from a holiday. I have a wonderful creamy wool blanket that I brought back from a trip to Morocco; it is more special to me than any mass-produced, run-of-the mill option. Textiles can be easy and light to tuck into your carry-on, and once home, you can make a few pillows, or simply drape a cloth over the back of a chair or sofa. Fill a basket with an assemblage of textiles to use as blankets on a chilly night. If you are more ambitious, think about a custom lampshade or curtains, or fashioning a dog bed with the fabric. India, Morocco, and Mexico City are some of my favorite places to pick up fabric. The diverse handicrafts are mind-blowing.

## ACCENTS

People often ask me about incorporating objects from travel and how to apply this to their interiors. My advice is with accents. There is always a space for something exotic in every home. Maybe it is artwork, a tribal mask, or an interesting textile to cover a chair or use to make a throw pillow. By thinking about the objects and giving them a new home in a different environment, they can feel fresh and contemporary. When you collect, look for things that have quality and a story. These are not items from the airport or hotel gift shops. The idea of collections may even seem out-dated, but I find that people gravitate toward the concept, simply in a more current way. Contemporary photography is a great way to start. The key is to not just buy anything, but something that touches you.

## LAYERING

Mix it up—provenances, styles, eras. There is nothing wrong with living in a home that emulates a *Mad Men* set, filled with vintage mid-century furnishings. But I tend to prefer a more layered look. From Parsons tables to a vintage French chair, classics can ground a space of any era. Mixing contemporary with classic makes things feel more current. I find a room filled entirely of antiques to be too much—like stepping back into your grandmother's home. When you have a tension of styles, with opposites attracting, it feels balanced. Adding in objects that are made by hand is a nice juxtaposition against articles that are mass produced. I once helped a friend who moved from the West Coast to the East, and the goal was to create a space that felt unique and layered. Instead of purchasing the dining room table from a large retail store, we had commissioned one by a local artisan. Going this route not only provided an interesting layer to the room, but it resulted in something beautiful to look at that also supported her new community. Don't assume that commissioning a piece means you'll spend a lot more. In this instance, the dining room table turned out to be less expensive than the retail option she had her eye on. Other perks of having it custom made? The reclaimed wood was from a salvaged barn, and she could choose the size that would work perfectly in her home.

opposite left: Fresh flowers are a must in my own house. I make a habit of always picking up something when going grocery shopping. And there's no need to complicate things: stick to one variety or color.

opposite right: Gathering objects like stones or shells from a walk on the beach can yield the easiest tabletop decorations. This was from a dinner party in Maine that I put together in just a few minutes.

below: Graphic patterns work together. This combination of geometric and animal print provides a good example. I think of the animal print as having a fluid quality, which contrasts to the uniformity of the geometric print.

# Parting Words

"Decorating is not about making stage sets, it's not about making pretty pictures for the magazine; it's really about creating a quality of life, a beauty that nourishes the soul."

Albert Hadley

I hope I have helped you attain the confidence to achieve the look that you desire for your home. My philosophy is that the home is the ultimate reflection of personality. I chose the title *The Curated Home: A Fresh Take On Tradition* to reflect this view: that the process of designing your home interior is one of collecting and interweaving pieces that reflect you as an individual. We are all influenced by tradition, but this does not mean our choices should be weighed down by the past. My goal is to provide you the tools to layer and meld elements of tradition with contemporary items to achieve effortless beauty, ultimately creating a home that you love.

# Acknowledgments

Many people have been a part of my personal and professional development. Without all of your willingness to listen to my ideas and dreams, none of this would be possible. I thank you for your friendship and support.

My San Francisco family: Suzanna, Sally, Richard, Valera, and Dorrit. From flea markets to adventures traveling the world. In the words of Auntie Suzanna, "Too, too divine!"

My New York family: Marsha, Allyn, and Stephanie. My home away from home. Thank you for always welcoming me with open arms and having every takeout menu in Manhattan. We miss you, Stanley.

My Florida and Maine family: Camille and Chick, with whom I can be completely myself, laughing so hard that I cry. Thank you for introducing me to the beauty of Maine.

Cece and the entire Scoppettone and Puentes families: for your love and support.

To my father and Chloe. As I mention in the Introduction, your early influence made me who I am today.

To my mother, whom I miss and think about every day.

Judy and Bob, who have created a perfect life that I admire. You're always supportive of my dreams.

Beatrice, the importance of your care in my early years can't be overstated.

I couldn't do any of this without my talented team at Grant K. Gibson Interior Design. You all continue to inspire me every day. Kelsey, you are my right and left hands. Cassandra, your creativity is inspiring. Chris, you keep everything behind the scenes in order. And from the past: Erin, Sara, Mead, and Kim.

Anh-Minh Le, my wordsmith: Thank you for every edit, text, and meeting. You have always taken my words and turned them into something wonderful.

My graphic and web designer, Sarah: You always listen to my vision and create designs that surpass my expectations.

Paige, the first editor to write about me who fast became a friend. So many years later now, your friendship and support mean so much to me.

Brian, a brother to me. It's been so great to watch you grow and evolve over the years. Seeing all you've accomplished puts a smile on my face.

Carolyn, my number one cheerleader and SoulCycle soul mate: I love having you in my life. And Wesley agrees!

My oldest friend, Sharon, whom I have known since kindergarten: letter writing before there was email. The mother to my godchildren, Elliot and Maisie.

All of the magic that you see on the pages hasn't happened without so many vendors and fabricators who have made our projects come to life. Showrooms, architects, contractors, painters, and upholstery and drapery workrooms.

Special thanks to Andrea, who perfects the finishing touches on every project.

The biggest thank you to all of my clients who trusted our firm to decorate your homes over the years. Thank you for allowing us to express our creativity.

Katie Killebrew and the entire team at Gibbs Smith: Every part of this book process has been a delight. You have turned the dream of a book into a reality.

To my photographer, Kathryn MacDonald: This book really is a compilation of our fourteen years of working together—a collaboration that could not have been realized without your exacting eye, capturing my work perfectly.

Lastly, Wallace and Campbell, my special Westie boys. I miss you every day.

# About the Author

Since launching his namesake interior design practice in 2002, Grant K. Gibson has guided clients through the often challenging process of reinventing their homes. His debut book, *The Curated Home: A Fresh Take on Tradition*, imparts insight into his approach—from his early influences; to the questions to ask yourself and vendors before embarking on a project; to his much-lauded designs that have earned him a place on *Elle Decor*'s A-list. Over the years, interiors that are traditional—but with unexpected eclectic and at times bold elements—have become a hallmark of his work. With this book, Grant hopes to provide readers with the inspiration as well as the foundation to see their own spaces in a new light.